# MAP
## Symbols,
## Keys,
## and Scales

by Susan Ahmadi Hansen

PEBBLE
a capstone imprint

Published by Pebble, an imprint of Capstone
1710 Roe Crest Drive, North Mankato, Minnesota 56003
capstonepub.com

Library of Congress Cataloging-in-Publication Data
Names: Hansen, Susan Ahmadi, author.
Title: Map symbols, keys, and scales / by Susan Ahmadi Hansen.
Description: North Mankato, Minnesota : Pebble, 2023. | Series: On the map |
Includes bibliographical references and index. | Audience: Ages 5-8 | Audience:
Grades K-1 | Summary: "Why are there stars next to some cities on a map?
What's that ruler in the corner for? Learn about the different parts of a map
so you can find what you need-whether it's buried treasure or your way to the
zoo! This first introduction to decoding maps will help kids build visual literacy
skills and navigate their world"-- Provided by publisher.
Identifiers: LCCN 2022001116 (print) | LCCN 2022001117 (ebook) |
   ISBN 9781666349634 (hardcover) | ISBN 9781666349672 (paperback) |
   ISBN 9781666349719 (pdf) | ISBN 9781666349795 (kindle edition)
Subjects: LCSH: Map reading--Juvenile literature.
Classification: LCC GA130 .H29 2023 (print) | LCC GA130 (ebook) | DDC
912.01/48--dc23/eng20220711
LC record available at https://lccn.loc.gov/2022001116 LC ebook record
available at https://lccn.loc.gov/2022001117

Editorial Credits
Editor: Ericka Smith; Designer: Tracy Davies; Media Researcher: Svetlana
Zhurkin; Production Specialist: Katy LaVigne

Image Credits
Capstone: 7, 8, Karon Dubke, 5, 17, Maps.com, 11, 15, 21; Shutterstock:
aldebaran1, cover (disabled icon), AmazeinDesign, cover (building icon),
AmeliAU (map), cover (background), 1, Artalis, cover (scale), CNGVahid, cover
(plane and bell icons), cTermit, cover (thermometer icon), Cynthia Farmer, 6,
Hopewell, cover (bus and shopping cart icons), iofoto, 19, Kitnha, 12, Laenz,
cover (weather icons), Peter Hermes Furian, 13, Porcupen, 9

# TABLE OF CONTENTS

Words in **bold** are in the glossary.

# What Is a Map?

A map is like a picture of a place. It shows us what is there. We can learn a lot from a map. But first we have to understand its parts.

A map uses **symbols**, **keys**, and **scales** to tell us things about a place. Understanding a map is like figuring out a secret code.

5

## Symbols

Maps use symbols to show the important **features** of a place. Symbols stand for things like schools, mountains, or roads.

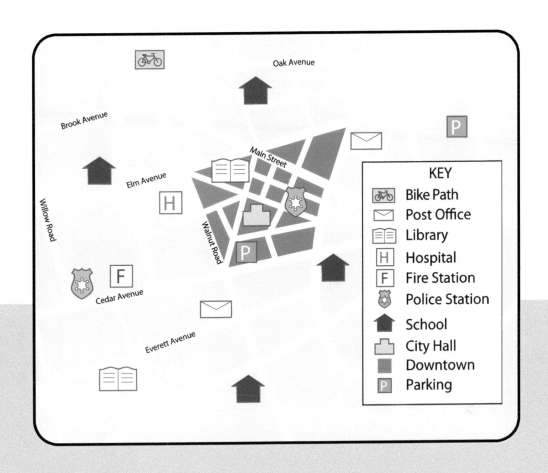

Maps use symbols to fit a lot of information in a small space.

Maps use different kinds of symbols. Symbols can be shapes or pictures. Colors are symbols too. Blue can show water. Green might be a forest.

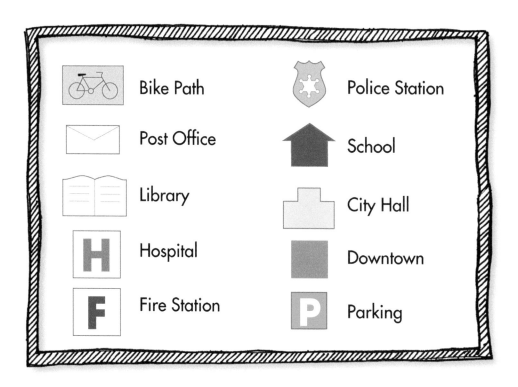

| | | | |
|---|---|---|---|
| 🚲 | Bike Path | 🛡 | Police Station |
| ✉ | Post Office | ⬆ | School |
| 📖 | Library | | City Hall |
| H | Hospital | | Downtown |
| F | Fire Station | P | Parking |

Lines can show **boundaries**. They separate things like countries. Lines can also show rivers and streets.

## Keys

Most maps have a key. It is usually found in the corner. Keys are also called legends.

Keys help us make sense of maps. A key will show the map's symbols. It explains what they mean.

# Yellowstone National Park

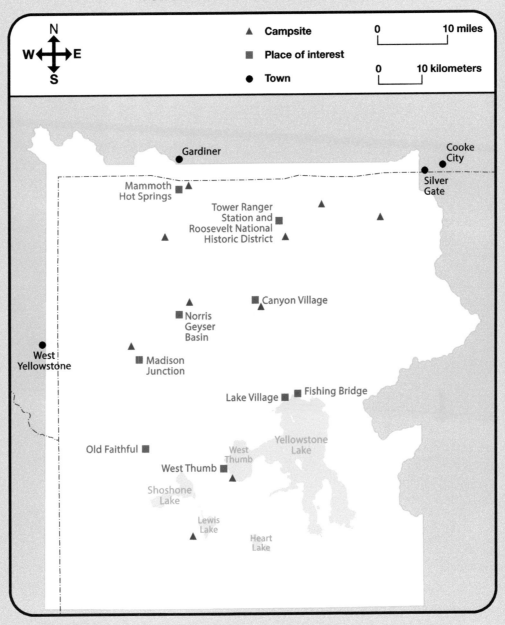

## Scales

The Earth is huge! How can it fit on a map? Mapmakers have to make things a lot smaller. They use scales to do it.

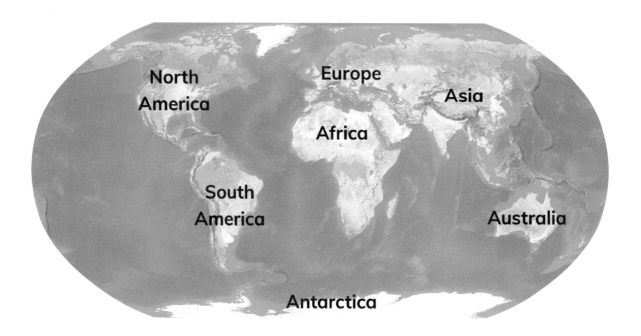

North America

Europe

Asia

Africa

South America

Australia

Antarctica

Some maps show large areas, like the United States. Others show smaller areas, like a park. Scales help us understand how big an area really is.

A scale can look like a ruler. One inch (2.5 centimeters) on a map might show 40 miles (64 kilometers).

A scale can also be written out. It might say "1 inch = 100 miles." Or it can be a **fraction**, like 1/1,000. This means 1 **unit** on the map is 1,000 units in the real world.

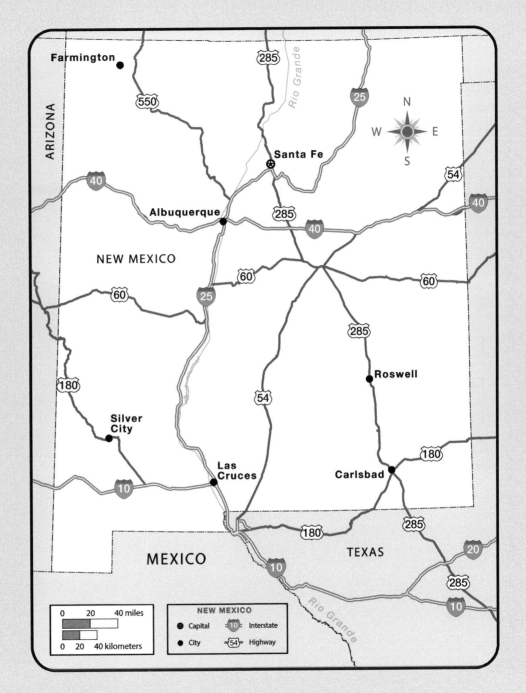

15

How do you use a scale? Get a ruler. Measure the distance between two places. Then, look at the scale. It will help you figure out the real distance.

Let's say the distance you measured is 5 inches (12.7 cm). The scale says that 1 inch is 100 miles. Multiply 100 miles by 5. The real distance is 500 miles (805 km).

## Using Maps

Maps teach us a lot about our world. Where is the closest school? Which states are next to Kansas? How far apart are Boise and Philadelphia?

Symbols, keys, and scales help us answer these questions and many more.

# Unlock the Secrets of a Map

Find a map of your state and a ruler. Use the symbols, the key, and the scale on your map to answer these questions about your state.

- What is the name of your state's capital?
- Find the city where you live. (Or find a city you know of in your state.) How far is it from the state capital?
- How many rivers are there in your state?
- What is the name of a park or forest in your state?

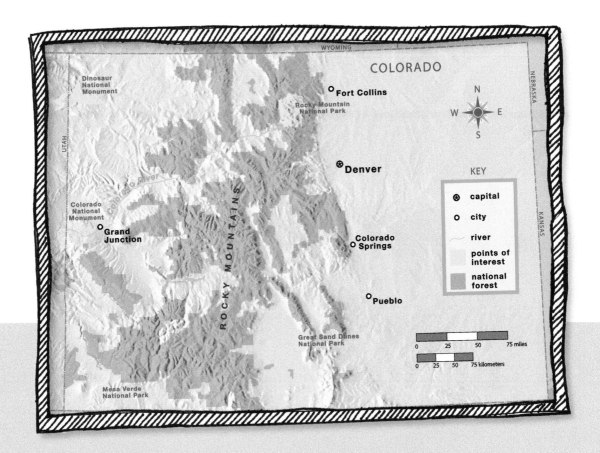

# Glossary

**boundary** (BOWN-duh-ree)—a border that separates one area from another

**feature** (FEE-chuhr)—an important part or quality of something

**fraction** (FRAK-shuhn)—one or more equal parts of a whole

**key** (KEE)—the words written beneath or beside a map to explain it; keys are also called legends

**scale** (SKALE)—a label on a map that compares the distances on the map and the actual distances on Earth

**symbol** (SIM-buhl)—a design or picture on a map that stands for something else

**unit** (YOO-nit)—an amount that is used to find the size of something

## Read More

Bell, Samantha. *Map Symbols and Scales*. Mankato, MN: Child's World, 2019.

Fanelli, Sara. *My Map Book*. New York: Harper, 2019.

Hansen, Susan Ahmadi. *Making Your Own Maps*. North Mankato, MN: Capstone, 2023.

## Internet Sites

*Britannica Kids: Map and Globe*
kids.britannica.com/kids/article/map-and-globe/353425

*Generation Genius: Read About Maps*
generationgenius.com/maps-of-earths-surface-reading-material

*National Geographic: How to Read Map Symbols*
kids.nationalgeographic.com/homework-help/article/how-to-read-map-symbols

## Index

## About the Author

Susan Ahmadi Hansen is a children's writer and a teacher. She especially enjoys teaching young readers and writers to fall in love with books. Susan has four adult children who live on three different continents. She lives with her husband in Cedar Park, Texas.